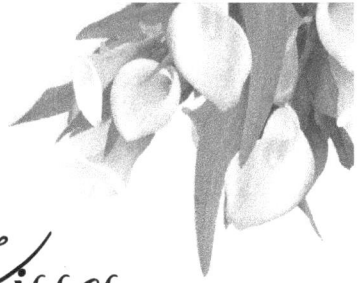

Love & Kisses, Final Wishes

Glenda A. Wallace

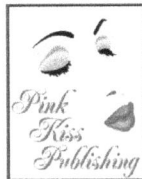

Pink Kiss Publishing Company
Gautier, Mississippi

*Scripture quotations are taken from the King James Version and the New American Standard Version of the Bible.

Cover by: Donna Osborn-Clark at creationsbydonna@gmail.com

Typesetting and Interior designed by:

glendawallace@pinkkisspublishing.com

ISBN 978-0-9835756-5-8

Library of Congress Control Number: 2012920207

Published by: Pink Kiss Publishing Company

P.O. Box 744

Gautier, Mississippi 39553

(228) 366-6829

www.pinkkisspublishing.com

Do not fear, for I am with you; Do not anxiously look about you, for I am your God. I will strengthen you, surely I will help you, Surely I will uphold you with My righteous right hand. — Isaiah 41:10

Contents

About the Book

One of the most difficult conversations to have with loved ones is about death and dying. No one really wants to talk about it. But no matter how unpleasant it may be, we must recognize that it is a reality.

For years I have been compiling my final wishes in order to simplify things for my loved ones in the event of my untimely passing. Everything they need to know is compiled in one place. My original plans for this book was to gift a copy to each of my loved ones so that they could also make their final wishes known and we could all be on one accord, but then I thought, *Why not share it with the world?*

"Love & Kisses, Final Wishes" is a guide for getting your personal and business affairs in order so that you can leave your loved ones with the greatest gift of all—Peace of Mind! It allows you the opportunity to prepare and provide the necessary information your loved ones will need at the time of your passing. But this book is so much more than that. It is also a keepsake that your loved ones will treasure long after you've departed this earth.

My greatest fear is not dying, it is unexpectedly leaving my loved ones saddened and grieving due to my death. So I want to make it simple for them to wrap up my personal and business affairs. I also want to comfort and reassure them with my words, and leave them with a keepsake, so that they can relive the special moments and highlights of my life.

Although this book is not a legal document, it can be used to assist your loved ones in carrying out your final wishes, but it should never be used as a substitute for legal documentation.

Important Tips

Fill out everything in ink so that it can't be modified or changed. If you need to make changes to any information already added, draw a single line through it and initial. There is a section at the back of the book where you can document any updated information if needed. Because this journal does contain a lot of confidential information, please keep it in a safe place. But remember to discuss with your loved ones where this journal will be kept.

And I heard a voice from heaven saying, "Write this: Blessed are the dead who die in the Lord from now on." "Blessed indeed," says the Spirit, "that they may rest from their labors, for their deeds follow them!" –Revelation 14:13

This book belongs to:

Name: _____

Legal Signature: _____

Date: _____

Personal Fact Sheet/ General Information

"Let not your hearts be troubled. Believe in God; believe also in me. In my Father's house are many rooms. If it were not so, would I have told you that I go to prepare a place for you? And if I go and prepare a place for you, I will come again and will take you to myself, that where I am you may be also. And you know the way to where I am going." —
John 14: 1-4

Name:

Date:

Address:

Phone Number: Cell:

Home:

Fax:

Office:

Date of Birth:

Place of Birth:

Social Security Number

Occupation:

Military Service Dates (if veteran)

Branch of Military:

Marital Status:

Name of Spouse:

Contact Phone Numbers for Spouse:

Address for Spouse:

Father's Name:

Father's Place of Birth:

Mother's Name:

Mother's Place of Birth:

Siblings: (names, addresses and phone numbers)

"And God will wipe away every tear from their eyes; there shall be no more death, nor sorrow, nor crying. There shall be no more pain, for the former things have passed away." — Revelation 21:4

Children: (names/addresses/phone numbers)

Grandchildren: (names/addresses/phone numbers)

Nieces and Nephews: (names/addresses/phone numbers)

Other relatives and/or friends to be notified:

14

Business Contacts to be notified:

Organizations affiliated with:

Religious Preference:

Church home: (name/address/phone number)

What to include in the obituary:

20

Resting Place

"This is my resting place forever; here I will dwell, for I have desired it. — Psalm 132:14

How would you like to be laid to rest? (select option below)

Burial:

Cremation:

What type of ceremony? (select option below)

Funeral:

Memorial Ceremony:

If burial, what location?

Is there a particular funeral home you'd like to use?

Preference of church:

If you'd like your body transported to another location (family home, different city, state, etc.,) list directions. Give as much detail as possible.

Wake, visitation, or family hours? Yes _____ No _____

If yes, are there any special instructions? _____

_____

_____

_____

_____

_____

_____

_____

_____

_____

_____

Open casket or closed? _____

Is there a preference for your officiant? _____

_____

_____

Who would you like to provide a eulogy? (List the name(s) below)

_____

_____

_____

_____

_____

_____

_____

_____

_____

_____

What are your favorite colors that you'd like incorporated into your ceremony?

_____

Any particular songs/music?

_____

Favorite scripture reading?

List any personal items you'd like to be buried with.

Would you like to be buried in your wedding rings?

If no, who should your jewelry go to?

Are there any particular pictures you would like used on the obituary or at the ceremony?

If applicable, would you like to be buried with your glasses on or off?

Would you like your own personal words read during the ceremony? If so, use the section below to include your readings.

What would you like engraved on your headstone?

Burial policies and locations: (If any)

Contact name and phone number of agent:

_____

_____

_____

_____

If cremation:

What type of ceremony?

_____

_____

_____

_____

_____

_____

_____

If opting for a funeral or memorial ceremony, do you wish your body to be cremated before or after the ceremony?

_____

_____

_____

_____

Do you wish your remains to be available for viewing during services?

_____

_____

_____

_____

How would you like your ashes disposed of? (select option below)

Kept in urn? _____

Scattered at specified location? (list location below)

_____

_____

_____

_____

_____

34

Wishes for Surviving Loved Ones

Although this is not a legal document, who would you like to care for your children?

If you have children, where do they attend school?

36

Who is their family doctor/dentist?

Where can all medical information be found?

Any know illnesses or allergies?

Any medications that they are taking or require?

40

Any special instructions for care of the child(ren)?

Location of any policies, college funds or trusts:

Pets:

Type?

Breed?

What brand of food do they eat?

What is the feeding schedule?

Who is the vet?

Where can medical information be found?

Any special instructions for care of the pet(s)?

Medical History

(Use this section to document any medical history/information that your surviving family members should know about.)

_____

_____

_____

_____

_____

_____

_____

_____

_____

_____

_____

_____

_____

Locations of Important Documents

(Remember to list locations of wills, health care directives, durable power of attorney for finances, safe deposit boxes, keys, bank accounts, direct deposit info, insurance policies, pensions, social security benefits, etc.)

56

Important Passwords

Financial Account Numbers

Verses of Comfort

Jesus said, "Now is your time of grief, but I will see you again and you will rejoice, and no one will take away your joy." - John 16:22

Blessed are you who weep now, for you will laugh. - Luke 6:21

I will turn their mourning into gladness; I will give them comfort and joy instead of sorrow. - Jeremiah 31:13

O LORD my God, I called to you for help and you healed me. - Psalm 30:2

This is the confidence we have in approaching God: that if we ask anything according to his will, he hears us. - 1 John 5:14

Let us then approach the throne of grace with confidence, so that we may receive mercy and find grace to help us in our time of need. - Hebrews 4:16

The LORD is my rock, my fortress and my deliverer; my God is my rock, in whom I take refuge. He is my shield and the horn of my salvation, my stronghold. - Psalm 18:2

My soul finds rest in God alone; my salvation comes from him. - Psalm 62:1

He who dwells in the shelter of the Most High will rest in the shadow of the Almighty. - Psalm 91:1

Peace I leave with you; my peace I give you. I do not give to you as the world gives. Do not let your hearts be troubled and do not be afraid. - John 14:27

I have told you these things, so that in me you may have peace. In this world you will have trouble. But take heart! I have overcome the world. - John 16:33

Keep me as the apple of your eye; hide me in the shadow of your wings. - Psalm 17:8

Restore to me the joy of your salvation and grant me a willing spirit, to sustain me. - Psalm 51:12

You are my hiding place; you will protect me from trouble and surround me with songs of deliverance. - Psalm 32:7

∿✚∾

Blessed are those who mourn, for they will be comforted. - Matthew 5:4

∿✚∾

I am still confident of this: I will see the goodness of the LORD in the land of the living. Wait for the LORD; be strong and take heart and wait for the LORD. - Psalm 27:13-14

∿✚∾

If you make the Most High your dwelling — even the LORD, who is my refuge- then no harm will befall you, no disaster will come near your tent. For he will command his angels concerning you to guard you in all your ways; they will lift you up in their hands, so that you will not strike your foot against a stone. - Psalm 91:9-12

∿✚∾

The LORD is my shepherd, I shall not be in want. He makes me lie down in green pastures, he leads me beside quiet waters, he restores my soul. He guides me in paths of righteousness for his name's sake. Even though I walk through the valley of the shadow of death, I will fear no evil, for you are with me; your rod and your staff, they comfort me. - Psalm 23:1-4

∿✚∾

I have fought a good fight, I have finished my course, I have kept the faith: Henceforth there is laid up for me a crown of righteousness which the Lord, the righteous judge, shall give me at that day: and not

to me only, but unto all them also that love His appearing. –2 Timothy 4:7-8

Praise be to the God and Father of our Lord Jesus Christ, whose great mercy gave us new birth into a living hope by the resurrection of Jesus Christ from the dead! The inheritance to which we are born is one that nothing can destroy or spoil or wither. 1Peter 1:3-4

Blessed are the dead who die in the Lord, says the Spirit. They will rest from their labors, and their deeds follow them. – Revelation 14:13

Jesus said, "Now is your time of grief, but I will see you again and you will rejoice, and no one will take away your joy." - John 16:22

Pieces of Me

(Use this section to share pieces of your life with your loved ones.)

78

Highlights of My Life

(Use this section to share special moments and highlights of your life.)

Favorite Photos

(Use this section to share your favorite photos.)

My Special Memories

(Use this section to share your special memories)

Letters to My Loved Ones

(Use this section to write letters to your loved ones)

114

126

128

130

144

150

176

200

218

216

214

212

Updated Information

(Use this section to update any outdated information through-out the book.)